For Nolan and Shane.

Amy the aging
Arctic alligator
always ate an appropriate
amount of anchovies
and apple pie
after an amazing
adventure abroad.

Benny the bearded
big belly beluga
had a blast
on his birthday
with his banjo
on a bright blue day
in the bay.

Cc

Cute and cuddly
Cat Sharks
Chloe and Carter
Can't quite contain
their curiosity when
Close to cans of
Congealed catnip.

Dependable Dorian
the daring dedicated
duck hunter
dives downstream daily
at dawn to deliver
delicacies directly
to downtown delis.

Enormous eyed elephants Eric and Emily eagerly eloped one eerie evening as everything around them exploded with earthshaking energy.

Funny Freddy
the fearless and
flatulent flying fish
frequently found that
he often farted
for fun.

Gg

Gary the goat guy
gladly gobbles
gallons of grape juice
with his green goblet
outside the giant
garlic garage that he
grew in his garden.

Henrietta is a happy hen who hops around the hills of her hay farm on her huge hairy horse hooves.

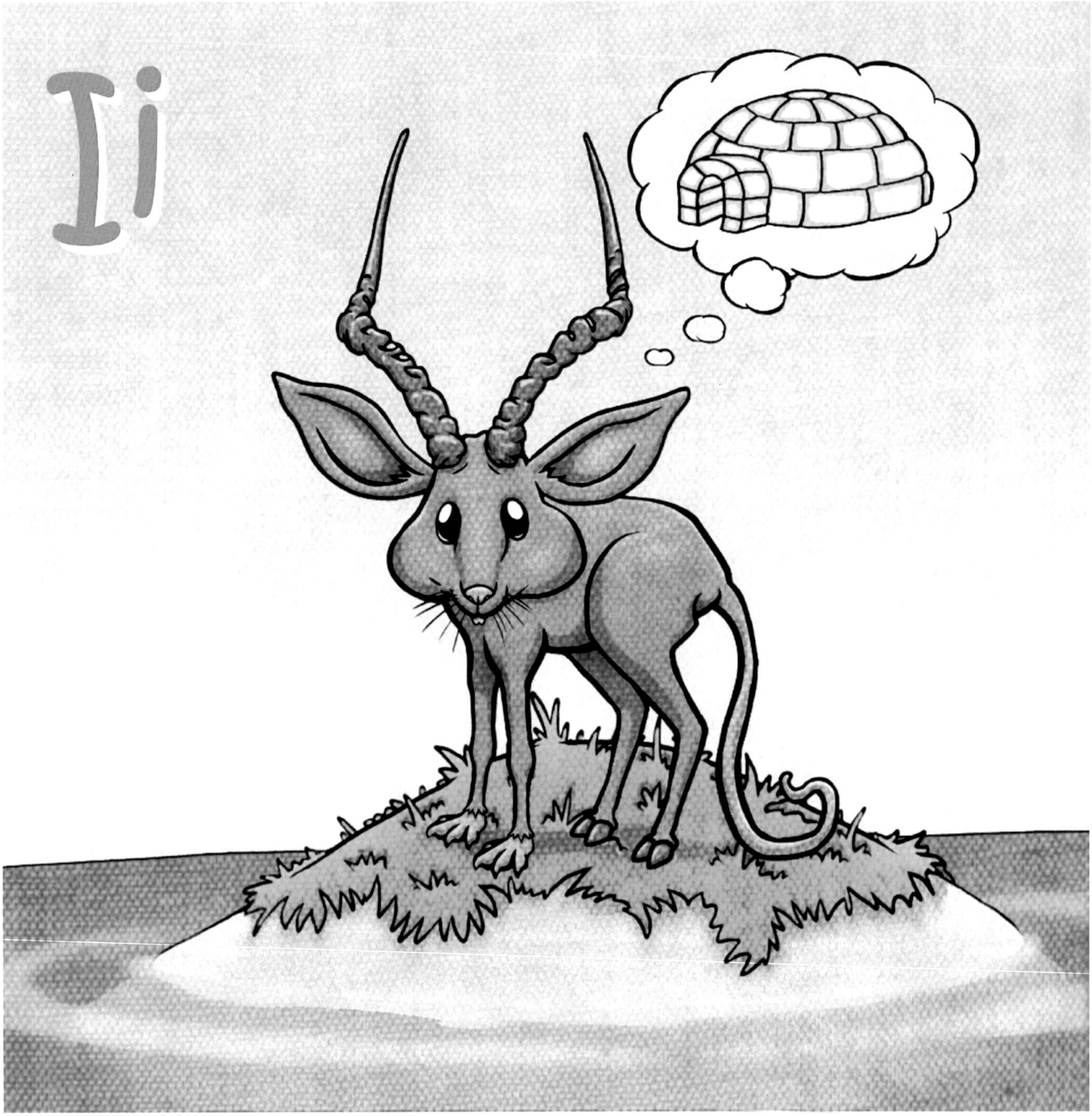
Ii

Introducing Ivan
an introverted
impala mouse
with the incredibly
idiotic idea of
importing ice to
include an igloo on
his itsy bitsy island.

Jolly juvenile
jellyfish Jon and Joey
jutted and jabbed
jumbo jalapenos
with their javelins.

Karen is the kind of kooky koalapillar that keeps her ketchup, keys, and kitchen knives in a kettle up in her Katsura tree.

Lucy the lovely
little lady lion
likes to lollygag as
she lugs around
luggage with her
lone lucky leg.

Mary the
marvelous and mighty
mountain mammoth
mustered up many
magic mushrooms
for a mouth-watering
moonlit meal.

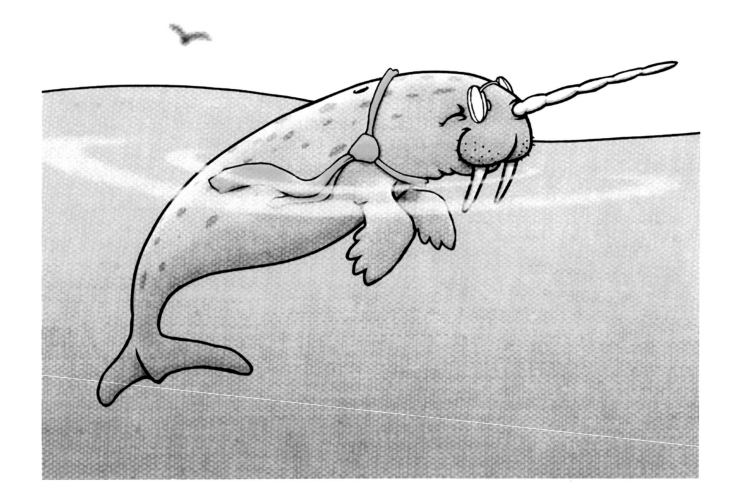

Nn

Nolan is a nice
nearsighted Narwhalrus
that normally needs
his new neon necktie
when he nods off
for a nap at noon.

Olivia the
obviously orange
Owligator observes
and obsesses over
her odd ornaments
up on her
old Oak tree.

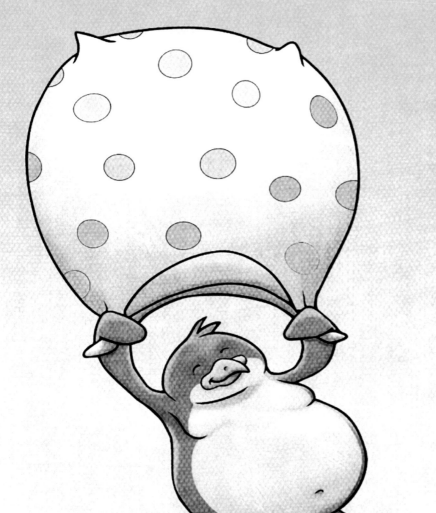

Pp

Pleasantly plump purple penguin Peter picked the perfect place to plummet with his poofy pink polka-dot pillowcase parachute.

Queen Qwimby
the quirky quail snail
quickly and quietly
crossed the quagmire
of quicksand.

Robin the rare
rusty red robotic
rhino really relaxes
in the refuge
of the retired
retro rocket range.

Say hi to Shane
a silly shy Shocktopus
that shocks sailors'
shoes and socks
that sink down
from ships on the
surface of the sea.

Tessa the tough
T-Rex Terrier
tried to tackle
the tennis ball that
her terrible trainer
threw through
the trees.

It was utterly unclear
and unbelievable
how Ulysses the
unicorn used his
unique umbrellas
to unicycle uphill.

Verona the valiant and vivacious vegan vampire whale voraciously devours various volumes of vegetable juice.

Weird and wise
Wolf Beetle William
wore his warmest
wrist watches to
wait within the wild
winter wonderland.

Xavier the
extreme X Ray
always experienced
anxiety examining
exotic fish
with his exquisite
X-Ray goggles.

Yy

Young Yanni the
Yak Bat yearns to
yo-yo yearlong
in the yard
of his yellow yurt.

Zach the zen zebra
zones out as he
zips and zooms
around the zoo
on his zany
zucchini zamboni.

71934830R00032

Made in the USA
Columbia, SC
07 June 2017